Mr. Pickett,
   You have been a
wonderful friend to Duane.
That has been a small training
ground for Parenting. May God
continue to Bless you and
your family.

Love, Cheers
Darlene
and the family

5/04

© 2004 by Barbour Publishing, Inc.

ISBN 1-59310-005-1

Cover design by Steve Bailey.

Published by Humble Creek, P.O. Box 719, Uhrichsville, Ohio 44683

Printed in China.
5 4 3 2 1

Why God
Made
Fathers

Conover Swofford

HUMBLECREEK
INSPIRATION FOR LIFE

God made fathers to show us different aspects of Himself. Our fathers are here to love us no matter what; to give us guidance down life's road (and this would include disciplining us); to be our good example; and to comfort us when we need comforting. Every father wants to make a better life for his children. He wants to help his children be the very best they can be. A truly wise father depends on his heavenly Father to help him accomplish the task of helping his children become respectable adults.

AN EARTHLY FATHER'S PRAYER TO HIS HEAVENLY FATHER:

My Father, I am so humbly grateful for my children whom You have given to me. I need Your help to bring them up in the way they should go. Help me to understand that each of them is an individual with special gifts and talents from You. Let me always look to You for guidance that I may guide them aright. Let me look to You as an example, that I may be a good example for them. Help me to teach them everything about You so they may know, love, and trust You as I do. And, Father, please keep their souls safe so that we may all be in heaven one day with You. Thank You, Father, for blessing me with my children, and please allow me to be a blessing to them. I ask this in Jesus' name. Amen.

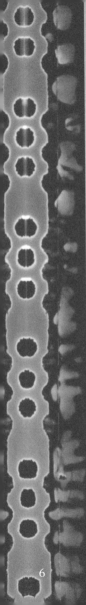

Because of you, my father,
I learned right from wrong;
I learned about the ways of God
And how to keep faith strong.
I learned honor and respect
And discipline from you.
I look at you and see
My heavenly Father shining through.

**I thank my God upon every
remembrance of you.**

Philippians 1:3 NKJV

There is no better example on earth than
a father who leads his children in the paths of righteousness.

Teach a child to choose the right path,
and when he is older he will remain upon it.

PROVERBS 22:6 TLB

One father is more than a hundred schoolmasters.

GEORGE HERBERT

Who can understand the importance of fathers? Our fathers provide for us, love us, give us someone to look up to, and teach us right from wrong. Our fathers make our homes secure and lead our families on the paths of righteousness. God gave us our earthly fathers so we can better understand Him—our heavenly Father. On Father's Day we honor our fathers, but we should honor them every day of the year.

Honor your father. . .
as the LORD your God has commanded you,
that your days may be long,
and that it may be well with you.

DEUTERONOMY 5:16 NKJV

Father:
A man who works as hard as he can
to provide the best he can
for those he loves the most.

A father teaches you all the important things in life—not just how to throw a ball but how to be a real person who does things right.

**Every father is a hero
in the eyes of his children.**

My father raised me in such a way
that I would rather face a horde of charging Huns
than to knowingly do something wrong
and see disappointment in my father's eyes.

My father's quiet,
"I wouldn't do that if I were you,"
carried more weight with me
than any other discipline.

It is a wise father that knows his own child.

WILLIAM SHAKESPEARE

In this day and age when fathers are ridiculed on TV and in the movies, we need to rise up and stand for the institute of fatherhood. Christian fathers are the backbone of our society. They are the strength of our families. They are the pillars of our communities. They are our examples. We need to honor them and respect them and love them. Instead of being our unsung heroes, we need to be singing their praises to the skies because they deserve our admiration.

The world needs Christian men today
To point us toward the light,
To set us an example
Of everything that's right.
God bless our fathers now, we pray,
As they do work for You;
And keep them safely in Your way
In all they say and do.

And these words, which I command you today, shall be in your heart. You shall teach them diligently to your children, and shall talk of them when you sit in your house, when you walk by the way, when you lie down, and when you rise up.

DEUTERONOMY 6:6–7 NKJV

Follow my example, as I follow the example of Christ.

1 CORINTHIANS 11:1 NIV

It behooves a father to be blameless
if he expects his son to be.

HOMER

**Father!
—to God Himself
we cannot give
a holier name.**

WILLIAM WORDSWORTH

The quiet, guiding words
a father has with his children
will be broadcast to the world
in their actions.

As soon as someone finds out that I have a foster father, their first reaction is, "Oh, so he's not your *real* father." My real father is the father of my heart—the father who has always encouraged me, loved me, been there for me. My real father is the father to whom I can tell my dreams and instead of ridiculing them, he gives me good advice on how to make them come true. My real father is the father I call to share my joys and my sorrows. To every person who tries to tell me he's not my real father, I have one reply, "If he's not real, how come you can see him?"

To have you as my dad
has been one of the greatest gifts
God has ever given me.

God gave us our fathers
so that we can see
our heavenly Father in them.

A father who is a good example
and someone to look up to
is one of the greatest blessings
God can bestow.

It is a scary thing for any father
to realize that his children
are walking in his footsteps.

And you, fathers,
do not provoke your children to wrath,
but bring them up in the training
and admonition of the Lord.

EPHESIANS 6:4 NKJV

A true father takes time to instill in his child the Christian virtues that child needs. The child may rebel and resent and chafe against that instruction, but when that child is an adult, he will appreciate having the strong moral background upon which to build a life. Adults who have no such background are like rudderless ships on the sea of life. It is a true father who helps his child become a responsible, caring adult.

A father is someone who gives you
the same advice he ignored when
his father gave it to him.

A wise son makes a glad father.

PROVERBS 10:1 NKJV

My father's gentle advice has shaped my life
into what I am today.

Just like our forefathers were the pioneers
who made our country great,
so our fathers are the pioneers
who pave the way to a better life for us.

Fathers were given to us
to show us the business of living.

"For I have known him,
in order that he may command
his children and his household after him,
that they keep the way of the LORD,
to do righteousness and justice."

GENESIS 18:19 NKJV

When I was fourteen years old, my father was so ignorant
I hated to have the old man around.
But when I was twenty-one,
I was astonished to see how much my father
had learned in seven years.

MARK TWAIN

**Becoming a father is easy enough,
But being one can be rough.**

WILHELM BUSCH

It takes a strong
sense of humor
to be a father.

He that will have his son have a respect for him
and his orders, must himself have
a great reverence for his son.

JOHN LOCKE

The proudest moment in my life
was when I knew that my father
respected the person I am.

My father always treats me as an individual.
He respects my wishes and feelings,
and in return I respect his.

Fathers are the spiritual backbone of the family.
It was my father who taught me right from wrong
by showing me his own faith in action.
More than just telling me how to be,
my father showed me how to be by his own life.

**I have no greater joy
than to hear that
my children walk in truth.**

3 JOHN 4 NKJV

21

Correct your son, and he will give you rest;
yes, he will give delight to your soul.

PROVERBS 29:17 NKJV

The awesome responsibility
that a father has toward his children
includes teaching them to discipline themselves.

**A child never looks up to anyone more
than he looks up to his dad.**

Just by living his own life, my father taught me the true
meaning of humility. Humility is not weakness; it is
strength under control. No one ever thought my dad was a
weak man. In fact he was universally admired for his
strength of character. Dad taught me more by being than
anyone else ever did by preaching.

**Fathers are always there
when you need them.**

As I look back on my life,
I can see the subtle influence of
my father's guiding hand
in all that I have become.

One of the dearest treasures I own is an old Bible of my dad's. Dad always made his own notes in his Bibles, and as I read this Bible, I learn valuable truths from the insights that my dad has had. This is just one more way that my dad can share his wisdom and knowledge with me, and I found that this made a very special bond between us that most fathers and children don't get to share. I wish more fathers paid attention to the spiritual side of their children's lives. I have always felt blessed that my dad cared enough about his children to teach us the most important things in life, and I thank the heavenly Father every day for my dad.

Father:
A loving hand outstretched to lead his children
in the ways of righteousness.

I want to live in such a way that
I don't hurt my father's feelings.

A quiet word, a helping hand,
a shoulder to cry on,
a gentle nudge in the right direction,
a loving heart—my dad.

To have a father pray over you—
to call the blessings of heaven down upon you,
to hold you up before the throne
of the heavenly Father,
to wrap the loving arms of prayer around you
and keep them there—
there is no greater joy or good.

fathers

There is nothing more tender than
a father's heart as he yearns over his children.

There is no comfort like
the comfort your father can give you.

**There is nothing like
having a father who
shares your dreams.**

I knew a man who was very shy, and almost everyone who knew him thought he was aloof. But his children knew better. They knew their father's heart, and they knew that they were in the very center of it. It doesn't matter what the world thinks of a man. What matters is what his children think of him.

There's no better feeling
than knowing you are in your father's heart
and that you always will be.

My father is a very traditional man. Every year on Christmas Eve he would gather us around him and read us the Christmas story from the Bible. Then he would pray the Father to bless each of us at Christmas and always. No matter where I am in the world, on Christmas Eve, I call my father and listen while he reads me the Christmas story and prays for me. I never have any better Christmas present than that.

CHRYS DANIELS

The character of the father is
echoed in his children.

The affection of a father and son is different:
the father loves the person of the son,
but the son loves the memory of the father.

ANONYMOUS

**A wise father also learns
from his children.**

29

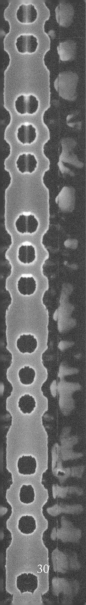

All of us wish our fathers to be like the father of the
Prodigal Son. We want to know that no matter what we do,
no matter how awful we are, no matter what trouble we've
gotten ourselves into that our fathers will still be there loving us and waiting to welcome us home with open arms;
not just forgiving us but rejoicing that we have come home.
How truly blessed are those of us who know we have such
fathers. Hopefully, we'll never test their ability to forgive us
but will know without the test that our fathers are always
willing to do just that—no matter what.

To err is human.
To forgive is a father's chief function
on this earth.

Heavenly Father,

Thank You for giving me an earthly father who shows me
so much of You. Thank You for his wisdom and intelligence
and loving heart; for his teachings and for his faith that he
shows me every day in the way he lives; for his kindness to
me and to others. Thank You for the good things he
instilled in me to help me be the best person I can be; for
his love for me and for letting him show me what a real
father is. He is very special to me, and I know he's special to
You. When I think of all the fathers I could have gotten,
I'm so very glad You gave me mine. Thank You
for my father, Lord. Please bless him as much
as he has blessed me. I am praying in the name
of Your Son, Jesus. Amen.

I know I'm one of the lucky ones

'Cause I got a father like you—

A father who taught me right from wrong

And other life lessons, too.

You're always there when I need you—

In good times and in bad.

You're not just my very best father;

You're also my very best dad.

I will open my mouth in a parable; I will utter dark
sayings of old, which we have heard and known,
and our fathers have told us. We will not hide them
from their children, telling to the generation to
come the praises of the LORD, and His strength and
His wonderful works that He has done.

PSALM 78:2–4 NKJV

> **Faith of our fathers,**
> **Holy faith!**
> **We will be true to thee till death.**
>
> FREDERICK FABER

It is a good thing for a child to have
the influence of both his parents.
A seven year old,
when asked why God made fathers, replied,
"To marry the mommies and have kids like me."
Children watch how their fathers treat their mothers.
Happy is the child whose father loves the mother
and lets the child know it.
A strong love between father and mother is
a sturdy foundation upon which to build a happy home
and to set the example of a good marriage.

Behold, children are a heritage from the LORD,
the fruit of the womb is a reward.
Like arrows in the hand of a warrior,
so are the children of one's youth.
Happy is the man who
has his quiver full of them.

PSALM 127:3–5 NKJV

A father has no greater joy than
to look on the face of his newly born child
for the very first time.

Fathers pass on many things to their children.
Some of them are physical, like hair color or the shape
of your ears. Some of them are emotional, like the
way you express yourself. Some of them are mental, like
an aptitude for math. Some of them are social, like how
you treat other people. Some of them are spiritual, like
a strong faith in the heavenly Father. But if you're
lucky, if you're really, really lucky, your father will pass
on to you something very special, like his passion for
double fudge chocolate chip brownies and his air of
innocent bewilderment when your mother demands
to know who ate them all.

No matter how old his children get,
a father never thinks his job is done.

**Happy fathers
make happy children.**

Nothing ever equals the scary thrill
of sitting on your father's shoulders
so you can see the parade as it passes by.

**The truly good fathers
rarely think they are.**

My father never yelled at us.
He gave us "The Look,"
and we knew we had better straighten up.
We almost wished he had yelled.

THE FIVE MOST IMPORTANT THINGS
A FATHER CAN DO:

1. Love your children
2. Discipline them
3. Teach them right from wrong
4. Be a good example
5. Respect them

The Best Father in the World

I know a man who is the best father in the world. His children love him dearly. He has set them the best example he knows how. He has taught them all he knows. He has nurtured their dreams and fostered their plans. He has given them every kind of help he knows how to give. He has instilled in them a strong faith in the heavenly Father above. He has loved them and taught them to laugh at themselves when they need to quit taking themselves so seriously. He has taught them about life by showing them how to live it. And he doesn't think that he's anything special. But I do. Because, lucky me, he's my dad.